ISBN 978-0-656-95750-7
PIBN 10499692

OF THE

GRAND COUNCIL

OF THE

UNION LEAGUE OF AMERICA.

FOR THE

STATE OF CALIFORNIA

AT ITS

ANNUAL SESSION,

Held in San Francisco, August 4th and 5th, 1863.

TOGETHER WITH

**A REPORT OF ITS TRANSACTIONS SINCE ITS ORGANIZATION,
APRIL 13th, 1863.**

SAN FRANCISCO:
PUBLISHED BY ORDER OF THE GRAND COUNCIL,
1863.

OFFICERS.

PROCEEDINGS.

IN GRAND COUNCIL,
SAN FRANCISCO, Aug. 4th, 1863.

The Grand Council of the Union League of America for the State of California assembled this day pursuant to call.

Present.— Messrs. Parker, Sherman, McLean, Clark, Pease, Dame, Chenery, Lull, Pacheco, Rice, Barstow, Holland, Allen, Dwinelle, Abell, Winans, Low, Taylor, McClatchy, Burton, Newcomb, Cobb, Dalton, Billings, Haswell, Gorham, Coffin, Rowley, Stevens, Cavis, Solts, Hilliard, White, Pinkham, Loucks, Pollock, Benton, Perry, Spalding, Smith, Reed, Mann, Taft, Pennell, Abbe, Michelhausen, Soher, Sprague, McGrew, Chandler, Sherwood, Perkins, McMurtry, Seymour, Rood, Henderson, Rider, Darling, Dyer, Young, West, Cutter, Drake, Cox, Aldrich, Hyde, Easterby, Shepard, Richardson, Markley, and Schuyler.

Grand President Parker in the chair.

Rev. J. E. Benton read the prayer from the Ritual.

Secretary read the call for the meeting of the Grand Council, as follows:

Grand Council of the Union League of America
For the State of California.
San Francisco, ——, 1863.
To the President of —— Council, No. —, Located at —— County of ——.

SIR—There will be a meeting of the Grand Council U. L. A. for California, at the city and county of San Francisco on Tuesday, the 4th day of August next, at which it is hoped, every Council in the State will be represented.

Those Councils therefore that have not already done so will please elect their delegates to the Grand Council and report the same at once to the Grand Secretary.

It is expected that the delegates from the various Subordinate Councils will be prepared to make an exact and minute report of the strength and condition of their respective Councils, the vote of the precinct where the same is located, and its probable division at the coming election. Such reports will state particularly the military capacity of the respective Councils with reference to the organized Militia and the Home Guard.

As no proxies are allowed in the Grand Council, those delegates who will be unable to attend the meeting are respectfully requested to resign their positions and thus allow their respective Councils to elect delegates who will be able to be present.

Only those Councils that have received their Charters will be allowed to be represented in the Grand Council, and those Subordinate Councils that are now working under Dispensations are requested to report immediately to the Grand Secretary and receive their Charters.

By order of the Grand Council.   Respectfully,

—— ——, Grand President.

—— ——, Grand Secretary.

Secretary then read the Grand Charter.

Mr. Chenery, from Committee on Credentials appointed at a previous meeting of the Grand Council, made the following report:

Mr. President: Your Committee on Credentials appointed at a previous meeting of the Grand Council have attended to the duty assigned them, and ask leave to report the names of the following delegates as entitled to seats in this Council, viz:

James McClatchy................Sacramento Council, No. 2
C. O. Burton.,..................Stockton   "   3
W. Newcomb..................Oakland   "   4
J. C. Cobb ....San José   6

D. F. Dalton	Santa Rosa	Conneil, No.	8
J. M. Billings	Santa Clara	"	11
C. S. Haswell	Nicolaus	"	12
Josiah Gorham	Woodbridge		13
O. C. Coffin	Martinez		16
A. B. Rowley	Alviso	..	17
J. E. Stevens	Yuba City		19
J. M. Cavis	Columbia		21
W. K. Solts	Suisun		24
F. Hilliard	San Luis Obispo	"	25
Wm. White	Santa Cruz		26
J. F. Pinkham	Placerville		28
Geo. P. Loucks	Pacheco		30
James Pollock	Benicia		31
J. E. Benton	Folsom		33
E. T. Perry	Meridian		35
Charles Spalding	Colusa		36
Wm. Smith	Bloomfield		37
Thomas Reed	Eagle		41
P. J. Mann	Crescent City	"	42
P. M. Taft	Jackson		43
L. A. Pennell	Upper Placerville	"	44
S. K. Abbe	Butte Creek		48
H. Michelhausen	Ukiah City		49
C. N. Fox	Redwood City	"	51
Joel Russell	Hayward		52
Lewis Soher	Mokelumne Hill	"	57
Thomas Sprague	Santa Barbara	"	61
Wm. H. McGrew	Noyo		65
J. L. Chandler	Mayfield		66
T. J. Sherwood	Marysville		67
John A. Perkins	Gilroy		69
W. S. McMurtry	Lexington		70
B. N. Seymour	Alvarado		71
A. N. Rood	Lincoln		72
J. W. Henderson	Cloverdale		74
W. M. Rider	Sebastopol	"	75
E. Darling	Little York Township		77

Barlow Dyer	Robinson's Ferry Co l,	No.	80
James Young	Oroville	"	81
D. J. West	Antioch	"	86
S. L. Cutter, Jr.	Sonoma Valley	"	88
L. M. Drake	Campo Seco		90
Jordon Cox	Windsor		92
J. P. Ames	Ocean		94
J. L. Shannon	Clayton		97
Geo. D. Aldrich	Franklin		99
S. F. Hyde	Tremont		100
A. G. Easterby	Napa City		101
Joseph Shepard	Vallicita		102
H. Richardson	San Pablo		103
John Schuyler	Weaverville		108
A. J. Markley	Somersville		113

Respectfully submitted,

CHENERY, Chairman.

On motion the report was received and adopted.

The Grand President then delivered the following address:

Gentlemen of the Grand Council of California;

In pursuance of what is deemed the usage of the State Councils of this Order in the States and Territories upon the Atlantic side of the continent, I deem it my duty to address you at this time upon the position which we now occupy here, upon the Pacific side, premising what I have to suggest with a few remarks upon the origin and progress of the Union Leagues of America.

It is only a year since in the hour of despondency, and after the reverses to the Union armies, that a few tried Union men in the city of Washington deeming it necessary that some action should be had among Union men, of such a character, as to prevent the secret movements of Government and Union armies from being at once communicated to the enemy, determined upon the organization of a secret Union League. They were well aware of the fact that a secret society, known by the name of "The Knights of the Golden Circle," had been for years in existence in all the Rebellious States, whose avowed object was the destruction of the

American Union, and which was rapidly extending itself among the Copperheads of the Free States, and especially in the Northwest, the result of which, in the fall of 1862, was the Union reverses and the partial copperhead successes in the elections held in Ohio, Pennsylvania, New York and Illinois.

They also saw that if something was not done at once to prevent the spread of this pestiferous doctrine of secession, and to unite all true patriots by a firmer tie than mere party organizations, the Copperheads would have the control of the next Congress, and the country would be lost.

Under this state of things the Union League of America was instituted, and the organization extended throughout the loyal States. The change in public opinion in favor of Liberty and Union one and inseperable, now and forever, became manifest throughout the length and breadth of the land; and the elections in Connecticut and New Hampshire held early in the present year first rolled back the tide of disunion which for a time seemed to threaten to engulph us all in the vortex of anarchy and political death; and it is to this institution, more than to all other influences, that we are indebted for this result.

On the return of our members of Congress from their labors at Washington, they brought with them the necessary documents, and on the thirteenth day of April, 1863, this Grand Council was installed by the Hon. T. G. Phelps, and has held regular weekly meetings from that time to the present. For a detailed statement of its work, I would refer you to the report of your Grand Secretary, Alfred Barstow, Esq., whose labors have been entirely devoted to the furtherance of the object of our institution since its establishment in this State.

Applications have been made to the Grand Council for the establishment of subordinate Councils of this Order in the Territories of Nevada and Washington and the State of Oregon. Dispensations have been granted for the same, subject however, to the action of the National Grand Council at its next session.

Some differences of opinion exist among the members of this Grand Council as to the secret character of the order, and it is often asked—1st, if resolutions adopted by a subordinate Council, in relation to public affairs, may be published in the newspapers;

2d, must the names of members be kept secret; 3d, may Subordinate Councils as such make public demonstrations; 4th, is the very existence of the institution to be kept from the public. Some judicious legislation upon this subject, which will secure uniformity in the working of the order, is very desirable.

It is sometimes asked if the members of the League are bound politically to support all the nominations of the Union party for State, district, county, and township officers, and if so, are there any exceptions to this rule? An answer from this Council would set at rest doubts that some entertain upon this important question.

By the returns that will be presented to you by the Grand Secretary, you will perceive the necessity for and capacity of the order for a more perfect military organization in this State among Union men; and when it is admitted that there are within the borders of our State some thirty thousand secessionists and rebel sympathizers, who are prepared upon the first opportunity to strike against the peace of the State and under the specious pretense of a Pacific Republic! create civil war and all its train of woes in our now peaceful homes, it well becomes us "in time of peace to prepare for war." I ask your most careful consideration of this important subject.

There is no doubt but what there is a large immigration to this State the present season across the plains, and that among them are hundreds, if not thousands, of disloyal men. Many of them may claim the right to vote in our State before having acquired the right to do so by a residence of six months as required by law.

Circulars have already been issued to the Councils throughout the State in relation to this matter; in fact, nearly all the matters to which I have called your attention, have already received some consideration from the Grand Council as organized by the resident charter members, but the full action of the entire State as represented by you would perhaps be more satisfactory to the Order at large.

It seems to me that the encouragement of Union newspapers, the spread of Union documents and speeches, the full discussion of patriotic questions, the formation of Union Clubs, the encouragement given to patriotic sentiment by song and music, the care of the wounded and distressed Union soldiers, are all proper subjects for our consideration in times like these.

In conclusion, allow me to congratulate you upon the success of your institution. In the four months of its organization more than one hundred Councils have been formed, comprising some twenty thousand members, who are true to the Constitution as it is, and the Union as one great republic established upon the broad ground of the Declaration of American Independence " that all men are created free and equal, and have certain inalienable rights among which are life, liberty, and the pursuit of happiness."

The Grand Secretary read the following transcript of the minutes of the Grand Council from its organization to the present time, and asked further time to make his report of the Subordinate Councils.

Report of the Grand Secretary of the Transactions of the Grand Council.

Mr. President:

At the invitation of Hon. T. G. Phelps a meeting was held in the city of San Francisco on the 13th day of April, A. D. 1863, to take into consideration the propriety of establishing a Grand Council of the Union League of America for the State of California. Mr. Phelps called the meeting to order and briefly stated its object.

The National Grand Council of the League at Washington had some time previously granted a dispensation to Dr. J. C. Bronson, of the United States Army, to establish the order in this State; but circumstances having prevented him from acting in the premises a dispensation was granted to Mr. Phelps.

After a full discussion it was resolved that the order be established in this State, and under the authority granted to Mr. Phelps the following named persons thereupon organized a Grand Council of the League for California:

T. G. Phelps,	T. Dame,
J. W. Osborn,	R. Chenery,
S. H. Parker,	J. C. Bronson,
Wm. Sherman,	A. P. Stanford,
John T. McLean,	C. T. Fay,
R. C. Drum,	Louis R. Lull
J. B. Thomas,	Wm. H. Parks,

Albert Dibblee,	R. Pacheco,
Jonas G. Clark,	B. W. Hathaway,
M. J. Burke,	E. N. Torrey,
E. T. Pease,	Jerome Rice,

Alfred Barstow.

On motion of Mr. Hathaway a committee of five was appointed by the Chair to report officers for the Grand Council.

Chair appointed Messrs. Sherman, Lull, Rice, Thomas, and Dame.

Committee reported as follows:

Grand President.—S. H. Parker.
Grand Vice Presidents.—J. W. Osborn and Wm. H. Parks.
Grand Secretary.—Alfred Barstow.
Grand Treasurer.—John Sime.
Grand Marshal.—M. J. Burke.
Grand Herald.—Jerome Rice.
Grand Sentinel.—Caleb T. Fay.

On motion the report was received.

Mr. Sime not being a member of the League the Chair decided the presentation of his name as Grand Treasurer as not in order.

The report was then amended by striking out the name of Mr. Sime.

On motion the committee to report officers were instructed to report the names of three additional Grand Vice Presidents and a Grand Treasurer.

Committee reported as follows:

Grand Vice Presidents.—R. Pacheco, E. N. Torrey, and Wm. Sherman.

Grand Treasurer,—Jonas G. Clark.

On motion the report as a whole was then received and adopted.·

On motion Messrs. Chenery, Lull, and Drum were appointed a committee to draft Constitution and By-Laws for the Grand Council.

On motion the initiation fee for membership in the Grand Council was fixed at ten dollars.

April 14th.—Grand Council met, and Mr. Chenery from committee on Constitution and By-Laws reported draft of Constitution, which on motion was received and laid on the table until the next meeting.

April 15th.—Grand Council met.
On motion of Mr. Lull, Nathaniel Holland was elected a member of the Grand Council.

On motion of Mr. Chenery, Thomas Starr King, E. S. Lacy, Frederick Billings, and R. G. Sneath were elected members of the Grand Council; and on motion of Mr. Fay, A. J. Pope was also elected a member of the Grand Council.

On motion of Mr. Dibblee the number of charter members of the Grand Council was limited to thirty-four.

On motion the report of the committee on Constitution was taken from the table, amended, and adopted, as follows:

"Constitution of the Grand Council of the Union League of America for the State of California.

NAME.

This organization shall be styled the Grand Council of the Union League of América for the State of California.

MEMBERSHIP.

The Grand State Council shall be composed of the thirty-four persons named in the Grand State Charter, and one delegate from each Subordinate Council in this State; nine of whom shall constitute a quorum for the transaction of business.

OFFICERS.

The officers of the Grand State Council shall consist of the Grand President, five Grand Vice Presidents, Grand Secretary, Grand Marshal, Grand Treasurer, Grand Herald and Grand Sentinel, who shall hold their offices for one year and until their successors are elected and qualified.

CHARTER.

All Charters for Subordinate Councils shall emanate from the

Grand Council, and shall be issued over the seal of the Council, and shall be signed by the Grand President and Grand Secretary. No Charter shall be granted except in open Council, and upon the application of one or more members of the League, or of a Subordinate Council.

DUTIES OF OFFICERS.

The Grand President shall preside at the meetings of the Council, and in his absence the senior Grand Vice President present.

The Grand Secretary shall keep a full and perfect record of the proceedings of the Council and prepare all charters. The correspondence of the Council shall be prepared by the Grand Secretary, and shall be over his signature and that of the Grand President.

Copies of all correspondence shall be kept by the Grand Secretary in a book procured for that purpose.

The Grand Treasurer shall receive all moneys and shall keep an accurate account of the same.

FEES.

The fee for a Charter and the Rituals necessary for a Subordinate Council shall be twenty dollars, to be collected by the recipient of said papers and paid to the Treasurer of the Grand Council.

PASS—WORD.

This Council shall have an independent pass-word, which shall be changed as often as the good of the League may require, and may adopt any forms, ceremonies, or regulations which may hereafter be deemed expedient.

REPORTS OF SUBORDINATE COUNCILS.

All Subordinate Councils shall report monthly to this Council. These reports shall include an exact statement of the number of members, names of officers, location, and such other particulars as may be deemed important to a correct and full knowledge of the condition of the League; also as to the strength and probable designs and movements of its enemies.

DISBURSEMENTS OF FUNDS.

All disbursements of funds shall be made by the Treasurer, by direction of the Council, on orders drawn by the Grand Secretary, and signed by that officer and by the Grand President.

BUSINESS DEMANDING SPECIAL ATTENTION.

All matters not provided for in this Constitution, and demanding, at any time, immediate attention, may be fully acted on by the Council at any regular meeting, or at any special meeting duly called—notice of which shall be given by the Grand Secretary.

MEETINGS.

Regular meetings of this Council shall be held on every Saturday evening; and special meetings may be called whenever the Grand President shall deem it necessary; and it shall be his duty, and in his absence the duty of the senior Grand Vice President present in the city, or Grand Secretary, to call a special meeting upon the written request of three members.

AMENDMENTS.

All amendments and additions to this Constitution shall be proposed in writing, and notice given thereof at least one week before action shall be had thereon. A two-thirds vote of the members present at a regular meeting shall be necessary for the adoption of any such amendment or alteration."

Mr. Lull was appointed a committee of one to report a pass word for the Grand Council.

Grand Secretary presented a form for charter for Subordinate Councils, and moved its adoption—carried.

April 18th.—Grand Council met.

Grand Secretary presented printed Constitution and Ritual, together with a seal for the Grand Council, which on motion were adopted.

Mr. Lull from committee on pass word reported the word —— as the pass word for the Grand Council.
Report received and adopted.

Messrs. Burke, Lull, and Barstow were appointed a committee to report a draft of circular letter of instructions to officers of Subordinate Councils.

On motion a charter was granted to Washington Council, No. 1, located at San Francisco.

On motion authority was granted to the President and Secretary to issue dispensations for the establishment of Subordinate Councils.

April 25th.—Grand Council met.

On motion charters were granted to:

Sacramento Council, No. 2, located at Sacramento.
Stockton Council, No. 3,   "   Stockton.
Oakland Council, No. 4,   "   Oakland, Alameda, Co.
Brooklyn Council, No. 5,   "   Brooklyn, Alameda, Co.
San José Council, No. 6,   "   San José, Santa Clara, Co.

The death of Grand Vice President J. W. Osborn was announced.

Mr. Fay presented the resignation of A. J. Pope, which on motion was received and accepted

The following named persons were then elected members of the Grand Council: C. L. Taylor, Edward Norton, L. H. Allen, and D. C. McRuer.

On motion of Mr. Holland, the sense of the Grand Council was taken upon the question of the eligibility of aliens for membership in the League, and the Council decided that under the Grand Charter they could not become members.

On motion of Mr. Fay, it was decided that aliens, having declared their intention in the proper Court to become citizens, were eligible to membership in the League.

Mr. Lull, from committee on circular letter of instructions, reported the following draft of letter, which on motion was received and adopted, and committee discharged:

Union League of America, State of California,
San Francisco, ——, 1863.

To the President of —— Council, No.—, U. L. A. :

SIR :—The Grand Council of the Union League for California

have instructed the undersigned to invoke the attention of the Presidents of the several Subordinate Councils of the League throughout the State, to the absolute necessity of observing inviolate the several pledges in the oath contained, especially those pertaining to committing to writing the signs, passwords, debates, or proceedings of any Council of the League.

And to the end that this necessity may the more effectually be impressed upon the minds of members, have adopted the following charge to be delivered by the Vice President to the candidates for membership, immediately after the administration of the oath.

Charge by the Vice President.

"GENTLEMEN :—Circumstances have arisen since the organization of the League in this State which, by a resolution of the Grand Council, render it my duty to charge you that under no circumstances is it consonant with the oath which you have just taken, to commit to writing any of the signs, passwords, debates, or proceedings of this or any other Council of the League of which you may become a member. A noncompliance with this obligation will render our association of no avail in preserving the Union, and will justly subject you to the distrust of all loyal men."

Enjoining upon you the imperative necessity of a strict compliance with this regulation of the Grand Council of the State League,

We remain, Gentlemen, very truly, yours,
By order.

——— ———, *Grand President.*
——— ———, *Grand Secretary.*

April 29th.   Grand Council met.

On motion charters were granted to
Petaluma Council, No. 7, located at Petaluma, Sonoma County.
Santa Rosa   "   8,   "·   Santa Rosa   "
Sotoyome   "   9,   "   Healdsburg   ''

May 2d.   Grand Council met.

On motion charters were granted to
Woodbridge Council, No. 13, Woodbridge, San Joaquin County.

Linden	"	15, Linden	"
San Luis Obispo	"	25, San Luis Obispo, San Luis O. Co.	
Woodland	"	32, Woodland, Yolo County.	
Georgetown	"	10, Georgetown, El Dorado County.	
Santa Clara	"	11, Santa Clara, Santa Clara	"
Folsom	"	33, Folsom, Sacramento	"

May 9th.—Grand Council met.

On motion charters were granted to

Nicolaus Council,	No. 12, located at Nicolaus, Sutter County.		
Yuba City	" 19,	"	Yuba City	"
Sonora	" 20,	"	Sonora, Tuolumne Co.
Columbia	" 21,	"	Columbia	"
Jamestown	" 22,	"	Jamestown	"
Chinese Camp	" 23,	"	Chinese Camp	"
Suisun	" 24,	"	Suisun, Solano County.

On motion the Grand President and Secretary were authorized to remit in whole, or in part, fees for charters in cases where the same should appear necessary and proper.

Messrs. Fay, Billings and Taylor were appointed a committee to report a draft of letter of instructions to Subordinate Councils.

May 16th.—Grand Council met.

On motion charters were granted to

Martinez	Council, No. 16, Martinez, Contra Costa County.	
Alviso	"	17, Alviso, Santa Clara	"
Coloma	"	18, Coloma, El Dorado	"
McCartysville	"	27, McCartysville, Santa Clara Co.	
Santa Cruz	"	26, Santa Cruz, Santa Cruz County.	
San Pablo	"	103, San Pablo, Contra Costa	"
Pacheco	"	30, Pacheco	"	"
Placerville	"	28, Placerville, El Dorado	"
Lafayette		14,	San Joaquin	"

Mr. Fay, from committee to draft letter of instructions to Subordinate Councils, presented a draft of letter which, was adopted as follows:

Grand Council of the Union League of America
For the State of California,

San Francisco, ———, 186

To the President of ——— Council, No.—, located at ———,
County of ———

Sir:—I am instructed by the Grand Council U. L. A. for California, to communicate to you the following resolutions adopted by the Grand Council on the sixteenth of May, 1863:

1st. *Resolved,* That no alien resident of this State is eligible for membership in the Union League, unless he shall have first duly declared his intention in the proper Court to become a citizen of the United States.

2d. *Resolved,* That Subordinate Councils be instructed not to initiate persons, non-residents of the locality where the application is made, unless the applicant shall make satisfactory proof that there is no Subordinate Council in the district or vicinity where he resides, and that he has not made application for admission to any other Council of the League in the United States; and also that no such initiation be made except when it shall appear necessary for the purpose of organizing Councils of the League in those sections of the State where the same do not already exist.

3d. *Resolved,* That Subordinate Councils be instructed to transmit immediately to the Grand Council the names of all persons rejected, and the cause of such rejection.

4th. *Resolved,* That all Subordinate Councils be advised to form within themselves a military organization.

5th. *Resolved,* That the officers of Subordinate Councils be advised to impress upon members the importance of never allowing private and personal considerations to influence, in the least degree, their action in balloting for new members; loyalty to the Government of the United States being the proper and only test for membership.

6th. *Resolved,* That Subordinate Councils be advised to make provision in their By-Laws for the impeachment of members who shall at any time be found guilty of disloyal or improper conduct.

You will please communicate the above to the Council under your jurisdiction, and take such steps as in your judgment shall appear necessary for carrying the suggestions herein contained into effect.

By order.　　　　Respectfully,

———— ————, Grand President.

———— ————, Grand Secretary.

May 23d.—Grand Council met.

On motion charters were granted to

Visalia Council,		No. 39, Visalia, Tulare County.
Putah Creek	"	40, Putah Creek, Yolo Co.
Eagle	"	41, Michigan Bar, Sacramento Co.
Bloomfield	"	37, Bloomfield, Sonoma County.
Crescent City	"	42, Crescent City, Del Norte County.
Benicia	"	31, Benicia, Solano "
Colusa	"	36, Colusa, Colusa ''
Meridian	"	35, Meridian, Sutter "
Grand Island	"	34, Grand Island, Sutter "
Jackson	"	43, Smith's Flat, El Dorado "
Upper Placerville	"	44, Upper Placerville " "
Watsonville	"	38, Watsonville, Santa Cruz "
Michigan Bluff	"	29, Michigan Bluff, Placer "

On motion, the Grand President and Secretary were instructed to grant a dispensation to W. E. Melville to establish Subordinate Councils of the League in Nevada Territory.

On motion of Mr. Clark, a salary of one hundred and fifty dollars per month was granted to the Grand Secretary.

On motion, a fine of two dollars and a half was levied on resident members of the Grand Council for absence from each regular meeting.

May 30th.—Grand Council met.

On motion charters were granted to

Yreka	Council,	No. 46, Yreka, Siskiyou County.
Farmingtown	"	47, Farmingtown, San Joaquin County.
Butte Creek	"	48, Butte Creek, Colusa "
Ukiah City	"	49, Ukiah City, Mendocino "

Pleasant Valley	"	50, Pleasant Valley, El Dorado	"
Alvarado	"	71, Alvarado, Alameda	"
Redwood City	"	51, Redwood City, San Mateo	"
· Hayward	"	52, Hayward's, Alameda	"
Virginia City	"	58, Virginia City, Nevada Territory	

Secretary presented resignation of Mr. Billings, which on motion was received and accepted.

On motion a committee of five was appointed upon military organization within the League, as follows: Messrs. Drum, Allen, Taylor, Lull, and Brannan.

June 6th.—Grand Council met.

On motion charters were granted to

Pilot Hill	Council, No.	53, Pilot Hill, El Dorado County.	
Montezuma	"	56, Montezuma, Tuolumne	"
Mayfield	"	66, Mayfield, Santa Clara	"
Arcata	"	54, Arcata, Humboldt	
Eureka	"	55, Eureka "	
Nevada	"	59, Nevada, Nevada	"
Little York Township	"	77, You Bet "	"
Moore's Flat	"	62, Moore's Flat "	
Mokelumne Hill	"	57, Mok. Hill, Tuolumne	"
Santa Barbara	"	61, Santa Barbara, St. Bar.	"
Marysville	"	67, Marysville, Yuba	"
Gilroy	"	69, Gilroy, Santa Clara	"
Mendocino	"	64, Mendocino City, Mend'o	"
Noyo	"	65, Noyo "	"
Auburn	"	68, Auburn, Placer	
Outside Creek	"	63, Outside Creek, Tulare	"

Mr. Drum, from committee on military organization, made a report which on motion was received and adopted, and Messrs. Drum, Allen, and Barstow were appointed a committee to draft a circular letter embracing the recommendations contained in the report.

June 12th.—Grand Council met.

On motion charters were granted to

Lexington Council,	No. 70, Lexington, Santa Clara County.	
Cloverdale "	74, Cloverdale, Sonoma "	
Sebastopol "	75, Anally " "	
Windsor	92, Windsor "	
Geyserville "	91, Geyserville "	
Knight's Landing "	76, Knight's Landing, Yolo "	
Dutch Flat "	73, Dutch Flat, Placer	
Lincoln "	72, Lincoln " ..	

Mr. Barstow, from committee to draft circular letter on military organization, reported the following draft of letter, which on motion was adopted :

Grand Council, Union League of America, State of California,
San Francisco, ——, 1863.

To the Officers and Members of the Union League within the State of California :

GENTLEMEN :—On the 16th day of May ult., the Grand Council issued a Circular Letter recommending the formation of a Military Organization within each Subordinate Council of the League in this State.

The necessity for such action has not diminished by time ; on the contrary, there is greater need to-day for the thorough organization of Union men than ever before. A determined effort is to be made at the coming election to array this State against the Administration and the War. To resist such an attempt we have pledged, each to the other, " our lives, our fortunes, and our sacred honor "—a pledge not idly made nor lightly to be broken.

In furtherance of the spirit of this pledge the Grand Council recommend :

First. That all able-bodied members of the League unite themselves with some company of the organized militia of the State. If there be no organized company of the militia at the place where the Subordinate Council is located, that one be immediately organized under the laws of the State, and an application made to the Adjutant-General of the State for arms. It is also recommended that those members of the League who, from age, infirmity, or other cause, are incapable of bearing arms, or who are unwilling to join the organized militia, form themselves into a Home Guard and perfect themselves in the drill by company and battalion, either using such arms as are accessible or without arms.

Second. Officers of Subordinate Councils will include, in their monthly reports to the Grand Council, the number of able-bodied men in their respective councils capable of enduring the fatigues of military service; as also, the number of those who from any cause are incapable; also, the names of those who have seen military service, when and where, and whether in the regular army, in foreign service, or in the organized militia of the State.

A vigorous effort is being made to induce the General Government to place at the disposal of the authorities of this State a quantity of arms sufficient to equip all whom in any contingency it may be necessary to call into service. Should this effort prove successful, notice will be transmitted immediately to all Subordinate Councils of the League in the State. An application will also be made for arms for such companies of Home Guards as shall organize themselves; but from the nature of the circumstances at present existing, without much hope of success—such companies will probably be obliged to supply their own arms and equipments.

Commending the suggestions herein contained to the consideration of the members of the League, we remain,

By order of the Grand Council.   Respectfully,

———— ————, Grand President.

———— ————, Grand Secretary.

Grand President and Secretary were appointed a committee with power to fix the time for holding a general meeting of the Grand Council, and the Secretary was instructed to issue a circular to each Subordinate Council notifying them to elect delegates where the same has not already been done.

June 26th.—Grand Council met.

On motion charters were granted to

Robinson's Ferry Council, No. 80, Robinson's Ferry, Calaveras Co.
Oro Fino Council, No. 79, Oro Fino, Siskiyou County.
Fort Jones   "   78, Fort Jones   "   "
Walnut Grove   "   83, Walnut Grove, Sacramento County.
Cacheville   84, Cacheville, Yolo County.

Diamond Springs "	82, Diamond Springs, El Dorado County.
Oroville "	81, Oroville, Butte County.
Excelsior "	107, Sutter Creek, Amador County.
Alleghany "	96, Alleghany, Sierra "

Secretary read the notice to Subordinate Councils in relation to meeting of 4th of August, which, on motion, was adopted, and the Secretary was instructed to forward a copy of the same to the Subordinate Councils and to persons holding Dispensations.

On motion Grand President Parker was appointed a committee to confer with General Wright and others upon the character of the immigration of the present season.

Resignation of Mr. Lacy presented and accepted.

Messrs. Alexander G. Abell, S. H. Dwinelle, Henry Carlton, Jr., and J. W. Winans were duly elected members of the Grand Council.

On motion it was resolved that resident members of the Grand Council who shall absent themselves from four successive regular meetings without permission of the Grand President shall cease to be members of the Council.

July 3d.—Grand Council met.

On motion charters were granted to

Damascus Council, No.	89, Damascus, Placer County.
Onisbo "	87, Onisbo, Sacramento "
Sonoma Valley "	88, Sonoma, Sonoma "
Campo Seco "	90, Campo Seco, Calaveras "
Los Angeles "	85, Los Angeles, Los Ang. "
Antioch "	86, Antioch, Contra Costa "

On motion the Secretary was instructed to extend to the Union State Central Committee such facilities in aid of the Union cause as might be in his power.

July 10th.—Grand Council met.

On motion charters were granted to

Aurora Council, No. 93, Aurora, Mono County.
Ocean " 94, Spanish Town, San Mateo County.
Occidental " 105, Angels, Calaveras "
Copperopolis " 106, Copperopolis " "
Vallicita " 102, Vallicita, "
Monitor " 104, Murphys, "

F. F. Low was elected a member of the Grand Council.

July 17th.—Grand Council met.

On motion charters were granted to
Last Chance Council, No. 95, Last Chance, Placer County.
Tremont " 100, Tremont, Solano "
Forest City " 98, Forest City, Sierra "
Clayton " 97, Clayton, Contra Costa "
Franklin 99, Virginia, Placer '
Napa City " 101, Napa City, Napa

Resignation of Henry Carlton, Jr. presented and accepted.

Grand President Parker from committee to confer with General Wright and others in relation to the character for loyalty of the immigration at the present season presented a report, which on motion was received and adopted, and the Secretary was instructed to prepare a circular embracing the substance of the report.

July 24th.—Grand Council met.

On motion charters were granted to
Weaverville Council, No. 108, Weaverville, Trinity County.
Centerville " 109, Centerville, Alameda "
Wilmington " 112, Wilmington, Los Angeles "
Sulphur Springs " 111, Sulphur Springs, Colusa "
Indian Valley " 110, Indian Valley " "
Somersville " 113, Somersville, Contra Costa "

Resignation of Mr. Sneath presented and accepted.

Grand Secretary was instructed to telegraph to the National Grand Council for authority to establish Subordinate Councils of the League in the States and Territories on the Pacific coast.

Dispensation granted to Elijah Steele to establish Subordinate Councils in Jackson County, Oregon.

Grand Secretary presented the following draft of letter on the immigration of the present season:

Union League of America, Grand Council for California.
San Francisco, July 24th, 1863.

To the Officers and Members of the Union League of America within the State of California:

GENTLEMEN :—Your attention is specially called to the following facts :

The Grand Council have ascertained from the best authority that about ten thousand male citizens of the United States are now on their way to this State, overland, at least three-fourths of whom are at heart rebels or sympathizers with the rebellion. These persons will attempt to vote at the coming election, and will succeed in doing so unless Section I of Article II of the Constitution (which is hereto appended) is rigidly enforced. This section requires an actual residence of six months in the State and thirty days in the county or district to entitle a person to vote. A mistaken idea has very generally obtained that a person's residence in this State dates from the time he left the Eastern States for California, and that our Supreme Court has so held. This is not true. Ex-Attorney-General S. C. Hastings, for certain purposes of his own, which he accomplished, gave as his opinion that such was a proper construction of the Constitution. His opinion is entitled to no more weight than the opinion of any other attorney, and is generally regarded by good lawyers as entirely erroneous and absurd.

It is possible that this vote, should it pass unchallenged, may determine the patriotic *status* of California for the next four years. Within that time the history of our Country will be made for centuries. No State in the Union can do more towards making glory of that history than can California. Our people to-day are loyal. Let not the dark brand of treason be stamped upon them by a failure to be vigilant. Let every Council appoint good men and true to attend the polls. Let every doubtful vote offered be challenged, and let a record be kept of every vote sworn in. Nine-tenths of the votes sworn in by the immigrants of this seasons will be rebel. At every precinct carried by such votes let the returns be contested. If this is done we are safe; if not, there is danger. We seek not to alarm; we only desire to impress upon all Union men the necessity for the same activity and zeal which is displayed by our army in the field. Let us remember that " eternal vigilance is the price of Liberty."

By order of the Grand Council.

—— ——, Grand President.

—— ——, Grand Secretary.

Constitution of California, Article II.—Right of Suffrage.

SECTION 1. Every white male citizen of the United States, and every white male citizen of Mexico who shall have elected to become a citizen of the United States under the treaty of peace exchanged and ratified at Queretaro on the thirtieth day of May, 1848, of the age of twenty-one years, who shall have been a resident of the State *six months next preceding the election and the county or district in which he claims his vote thirty days,* shall be entitled to vote at all elections which are now or hereafter may be authorized by law. * * * *

On motion, the circular was adopted and ordered forwarded to the various Councils of the State.

July 31st.—Grand Council met.

On motion charters were granted to
Somersville Council, No. 113, Somersville, Contra Costa County.
Forest City " 98, Forest City, Sierra "

Grand Secretary read telegram from the Grand President of the National Grand Council authorizing dispensations to be issued by the Grand Council for California within the States and Territories of the Pacific coast.

On motion Messrs. Chenery, Dwinelle, and Pease were appointed a committee on credentials for the meeting of August 4th.

Messrs. W. C. Ralston and W. B. Farwell were elected members of the Grand Council.

Respectfully submitted,
ALFRED BARSTOW,
Grand Secretary.

Report received and further time granted.

The Grand Treasurer presented the following report:

Mr. President:

I transmit herewith a report of all moneys received and disbursed since the organization of the Grand Council.

Respectfully,
JONAS G. CLARK,
Grand Treasurer.

SAN FRANCISCO, August 4th, 1863.

CASH.—Dr.

To fees for charters....................$1,315 00
To fees for initiation 260 00
To fines for non-attendance............. 100 00
                                         ————$1,675 00

CONTRA.—Cr.

By cash paid as per vouchers..... .... 1,230 75

Cash on hand............................. $444 25

On motion the report was received.

On motion of Mr. Stevens of Sutter the Grand President's address was referred to a committee of five.

Chair appointed Messrs. Stevens of Sutter, Burton of San Joaquin, McClatchy of Sacramento, Soher of Calaveras, and Rider of Sonoma.

Mr. Cutter of Sonoma moved that the Chair appoint a committee of five on Order of Business.—Carried.

Chair appointed Messrs. Cutter of Sonoma, Cobb of Santa Clara, Pinkham of El Dorado, Schuyler of Trinity, and Hilliard of San Luis Obispo.

Grand President gave the pass word of the Grand Council.

Mr. Lüll of San Francisco was appointed Secretary *pro tem.*

On motion of Mr. Holland of San Francisco, the Council went into committee of the whole on the state of the Order in California. Mr. Burton of San Joaquin in the Chair.

Mr. Parker of San Francisco reported on Council No. 1.

Mr. McClatchey of Sacramento, for Council No. 2.

Committee rose and had leave to sit again.

Mr. Cutter of Sonoma, from committee on order of business made the following report:

Mr. President: Your committee appointed upon order of business have had the same under consideration, and ask leave to report in part as follows, and ask further time:

Order of Business.

1st. The adoption of a Constitution for the Grand Council U. L. A. for California, recommending the one now published.

2d. Election of officers, singly and by ballot.

3d. Reports of the Grand Secretary and Grand Treasurer.

4th. General remarks from delegates upon the condition of their respective Councils; and

5th. Adjournment until 10 A. M. to-morrow, August 5th.

Respectfully submitted,
CUTTER, Chairman.

On motion the report was received, and committee granted further time.

On motion of Mr. Burton of San Joaquin, sections first and second, relating to the adoption of the constitution and the election of officers, were stricken out.

Section five was then amended so as to read: "5th. Adjournment until 9 o'clock, P. M. to-morrow, August 5th."

On motion the report as amended was then adopted.

On motion, Mr. Lull of San Francisco was added to the committee on order of business.

Grand Council went into committee of the whole, Mr. Benton of Folsom in the chair.

Mr. Burton of San Joaquin reported for Council, No. 3.
Mr. Newcomb of Alameda   "   "   4.
Mr. Cobb of Santa Clara   "   "   6.
Mr. Billings of Santa Clara   "   ..   11.
Mr. Haswell of Sutter   12.
Mr. Gorham of San Joaquin   "   13.
Mr. Coffin of Contra Costa   ..   16.
Mr. Rowley of Santa Clara   ..   17.
Mr. Stevens of Sutter   19.
Mr. Cavis of Tuolumne   ..   21.
Mr. Solts of Solano   ..   ..   24.
Mr. Hilliard of San Luis Obispo "   25.
Mr. White of Santa Cruz   "   ..   26.
Mr. Pinkham of El Dorado   "   ..   28.
Mr. Loucks of Contra Costa   "   30.
Mr. Pollock of Solano   ..   31.
Mr. Benton of Sacramento   ..   33.
Mr. Perry of Sutter   35.
Mr. Spalding of Colusa   ..   36.
Mr. Smith of Sonoma   ..   37.
Mr. Reed of Sacramento   ..   41.
Mr. Mann of Del Norte   ..   42.
Mr. Taft of El Dorado   ..   43.
Mr. Pennell of El Dorado   44.
Mr. Abbe of Colusa   ..   ..   48.
Mr. Michelhausen of Mendocino   "   ..   49.

Mr. Soher of Calaveras reported for Council, No. 57.
Mr. Sprague of Santa Barbara   "   "   61.
Mr. McGrew of Mendocino   "   "   65.
Mr. Chandler of Santa Clara   "   "   66.
Mr. Sherwood of Yuba   ..   67.
Mr. Perkins of Santa Clara   "   ..   69.
Mr. McMurtry of Santa Clara   "   70.
Mr. Seymour of Alameda   ..   71.
Mr. Rood of Placer   72.
Mr. Henderson of Sonoma   ..   74.
Mr. Rider of Sonoma   ..   75.
Mr. Darling of Nevada   ..   77.

Committee rose and had leave to sit again.

On motion adjourned.

ALFRED BARSTOW, Grand Secretary.

August 5th, 1863.

Grand Council met pursuant to adjournment.

Present—Messrs. Parker, Sherman, Barstow, Clark, Rice, Fay, Drum, Lull, Hathaway, Holland, Taylor, Winans, Low, McClatchy, Burton, Cobb, Dalton, Billings, Haswell, Gorham, Coffin, Rowley, Stevens, Cavis, Solts, Hilliard, White, Pinckham, Pollock, Benton, Perry, Spalding, Smith, Reed, Mann, Taft, Pennell, Abbe, Michelhausen, Fox, Russell, Soher, Sprague, McGrew, Chandler, Sherwood, Perkins, McMurtry, Seymour, Rood, Henderson, Rider, Darling, Dyer, Young, West, Cutter, Drake, Cox, Ames, Shannon, Aldrich, Hyde, Easterby, Shepard, Richardson, Schuyler, and Markley.

Grand President Parker in the chair.

Minutes of the previous meeting read an approved.

Committee on order of business made a further report, as follows:

Mr. President: Your committee on order of business would further report, as an order of business for the day:

1st. The appointment of a standing committee of five on resolutions.

2d. Report of committee on President's address.

3d. Introduction of Resolutions.

4th. Reports of Grand Secretary and Grand Treasurer.

5th. The transaction of miscellaneous business.

And ask to be discharged.

Respectfully submitted,
CUTTER, Chairman.

On motion, the report was received and adopted, and committee discharged.

Chair appointed committee on Resolutions as follows: Benton of Sacramento, Seymour of Alameda, Cobb of Santa Clara, Burton of San Joaquin, Taft of El Dorado.

Mr. Stevens, from committee on President's address, made the following report:

Mr. President, your committee, to whom was referred the Grand President's address, have carefully considered the matters and suggestions therein contained, and ask leave to report as follows:

That there should be differences of opinion touching the working policy of the organization *in times of peace* is naturally to be expected; and could we have assurances that the peace and quiet that now happily prevails in our State would remain unbroken, your committee believe that the necessity for a secret Union organization would not exist.

But the existence of the present formidable rebellion and the great number of rebel sympathizers in our midst render it necessary and proper for Union men to band together and work harmoniously and efficiently for the preservation of the Government bequeathed to them by their revolutionary fathers.

Believing, then, that our organization is calculated to further the object which all Union men have nearest their hearts, and that its efficiency and usefulness will be in proportion to the harmony which exists among its members and the uniformity of the action of the various Councils, your committee would reply to the questions and suggestions contained in the address in their order as follows:

First.—May resolutions adopted by a Subordinate Council in relation to public affairs be published in the newspapers as emanating from such Council?

This question is answered by the Ritual—No.

Second.—Must the names of the members be kept secret? No; but it is good policy to do so. It is a matter of discretion with the members.

Third.—May Subordinate Councils, as such, make public demonstrations?

No; but should aid as individual Union men.

Fourth.—Is the very existence of the organization to be kept secret?

Not necessarily.

Fifth.—Are members of the U. L. A. bound politically to support all the nominees of the Union party for State, district, county and township officers?

No; but they are bound to support *good and reliable Union men and no others*.

Your committee most heartily approve the suggestions of the Grand President relative to the propriety of Subordinate Councils aiding in the circulation of Union newspapers, documents, speeches, and the promotion of the success of Union demonstrations.

Your committee would further report that they feel incompetent, in the brief time allowed them, to make such report upon the military portion of the address as its importance demands and as the Grand Council have a right to expect at our hand, we therefore recommend that so much of the address as relates to military organization be referred to the committee on military organization, with instructions to report at the earliest practicable moment.

All of which is respectfully submitted,

STEVENS,

Chairman.

On motion the report was received and the committee discharged.

On motion the report of the committee was read by sections by Mr. Burton of San Joaquin.

On motion, section first was adopted as read.

Section second was then read and on motion so amended as to read as follows:

Second.—Must the names of members be kept secret?

Yes, so far as practicable.

Section three read and adopted.

Section four read and adopted.

Section five read and adopted.

The recommendations of the report were then approved, and on motion of Mr. Benton of Sacramento the report as amended was adopted as a whole and the committee discharged.

Chair announced the next order of business to be the introduction of resolutions.

Mr. McClatchy of Sacramento in the chair.

Mr. Rowley of Alviso introduced the following and moved its adoption:

Resolved, That a committee of three be appointed by the Chair to wait on General Wright immediately and request of him in the name of this Council to place at the disposition of the State authorities a sufficient quantity of arms, amunition, and equipments to arm and equip the organized militia of this State, and report his answer to the Grand Council.

After some debate the resolution was withdrawn by the mover.

Introduced by Mr. Holland of San Francisco:

Resolved, That Subordinate Councils of the League be authorized to publish loyal addresses that may be delivered before such Councils from time to time, under the supervision of this Grand Council: Provided, that this resolution be ratified by the National Grand Council U. L. A. at the city of Washington.

Referred to committee on resolutions. Resolution reported back and passage recommended.

On motion report of committee was adopted and resolution passed.

Introduced by Mr. McClatchy of Sacramento, by instruction of Council No. 2:

Resolved, That the names of all persons known to be disloyal in the respective districts of the Subordinate Councils be canvassed and collected, and reported to the Grand Council for the purpose of collating and publishing in book form such of them as it may deem advisable for future reference.

Referred to committee on resolutions. Reported back and passage recommended.

Amended by providing that, as far as possible, the occupation, age, and birth place shall be reported, together with the fact as to whether the persons named can read and write.

Resolution as amended adopted.

Upon suggestion of the Grand President, setting forth the necessity for some legislation in the premises,
Mr. Pinkham of El Dorado moved that a special committee of three be appointed by the Chair to take into consideration and report upon the expediency of allowing Subordinate Councils to adopt an independent pass word for their respective Councils.
Carried.

Chair appointed Messrs. Pinkham, McClatchy, and Rider.

Mr. McClatchy in the Chair.

Mr. Soher of Calaveras introduced the following resolution:

Resolved, That this Grand Council recommend that there be entire uniformity in the secret work of the League in all Subordinate Councils of the State. Adopted.

Introduced by Mr. West of Contra Costa :

Resolved, That the Grand Secretary be instructed to prepare and forward to all Subordinate Councils a quarterly report of the transactions of the Grand Council, with the names of persons refused admittance into the League, and such other information as he may have in his possession respecting the same. Adopted.

By Mr. Fox of San Mateo :

Resolved, That the President of each Subordinate Council is requested to confer with the Presidents of the adjoining Councils in each direction and, as far as practicable, so arrange the boundary of the territory in regard to which each Council shall report to the Grand Council that no two or more Councils shall report in reference to the same territory. Adopted.

By Mr. Darling of Nevada :

Resolved, That it is the duty of the Union men of California to place the State upon a war footing ; and we hereby recommend that all able bodied members of the Union League enroll themselves in the organized militia of the State. Adopted.

By Mr. Fox of San Mateo :

Resolved, That the Grand President be requested, at some time during the session of the Grand Council, to illustrate the secret work of the League or cause the same to be done. Adopted.

At 1 o'clock P. M., on motion of Mr. Lull of San Francisco, the Grand Council took a recess of thirty minutes.

Aug. 5th.—Grand Council reassembled. Grand President Parker in the chair.

Mr. Billings of Santa Clara introduced the following resolution :

Resolved, that this Council recommend to all Subordinate Councils to organize without delay open Union Clubs, and to procure the delivery of patriotic addresses, songs, etc. before them, and to labor earnestly for the success of the Union ticket at the coming election. Adopted.

The committee to whom was referred the subject matter of the Grand President's suggestion in relation to pass word, reported back the following resolution and recommended its passage.

Resolved 1st, That each Subordinate Council be authorized to adopt a quarterly pass word for the use of its own members; such pass word to be selected by a committee consisting of the President, Vice President, and Secretary.

2d. Upon the application of persons, not members of the Council, for admission, it shall be the duty of the President to appoint a committee of three, who shall examine such persons in the work of the order, and shall administer a test oath in regard to their membership and standing in the order. The committee shall then report the result of such examination to the Council, and if no objecobjection be made such persons shall be admitted upon giving the general pass word and observing the signs of admission.

3d. Members of the order may be admitted to Subordinate Councils of which they are not members upon being vouched for by any member of the Council in good standing.

4th. The form of the test oath to be taken by parties applying for admission to Councils of which they are not members, shall be as follows: " I do solemnly swear that I am a member of the Union League of America in good standing."

PINKHAM AND McCLATCHY, for Committee.

On motion the report of the committee was adopted and the resolution passed.

The Grand Secretary presented a report giving the statistics of the order as far as Subordinate Councils had reported, the number and names of persons refused admittance into the order, and the correspondence relative to the publication of speeches, resolutions, etc.

On motion the report was received.

Secretary read the resolution presented by Mr. Darling of Nevada and passed by the Grand Council in relation to placing the State upon a war footing, and Col. Drum stated to the Council that General Wright would take the responsibility of issuing arms to organized companies of the militia upon being satisfied of the responsibility and loyalty of the applicants.

On motion of the Secretary charters were granted to Poland Council, San Joaquin County, and to Lockford Council, San Joaquin County.

By request of the Grand President, Mr. Benton of Folsom Council gave the secret work of the order.

On motion, the work as given by Mr. Benton was declared correct and adopted, and delegates were instructed to see that the work of their respective Councils conformed to it.

Mr. Stevens moved that the proceedings of this meeting be published and transmitted to Subordinate Councils.

Mr. Lull moved as an amendment that the transactions of the Grand Council be published and forwarded to the National Grand Council and to the Subordinate Councils in this State. Amendment accepted.

Mr. Fox moved as a further amendment that it be left discretionary with the President and Secretary to publish such portion of the transactions as they should deem advisable. Amendment accepted and motion carried.

Mr. Holland of San Francisco, moved that the next annual meeting of the Grand Council be held on the first Tuesday of August, A. D. 1864, and that at that meeting officers of the Grand Council be elected.

Mr. Burton of Stockton, moved to amend by striking out August and inserting September.

Amendment adopted and motion carried.

On motion of Mr. Billings of Santa Clara, the Grand Council adjourned.

ALFRED BARSTOW, Grand Secretary.